A Harmony of the Gospels

A Chronological Study of Matthew, Mark, Luke & John

A series of questions designed to guide a study of the life of Christ from His preexistence to his ascension.

Compiled by Mark B. Pape

The outline for this study was patterned after
A Harmony of the Gospel by A. T. Robertson (1863-1934)

2015 One Stone Press.
All rights reserved. No part of this book may be reproduced
in any form without written permission of the publisher.

Published by:
One Stone Press
979 Lovers Lane
Bowling Green, KY 42103

Printed in the United States of America

ISBN 10:1-941422-14-4
ISBN 13:978-1-941422-14-4

Supplemental Materials Available:
Answer key
Downloadable PDF

www.onestone.com

Table of Contents

1. The Sources of the Gospels 5
2. The Pre-Existence, Incarnation and Genealogies of Jesus 7
3. The Birth of John the Baptist and Jesus and Their Childhood 9
4. The Beginning of Christ's Public Ministry 15
5. The Galilean Ministry 21
6. The Judean Ministry 55
7. The Perean Ministry 67
8. The Last Public Ministry in Jerusalem 81
9. The Last Few Days Before His Trial 89
10. The Arrest, Trial, Crucifixion and Burial of Jesus 97
11. The Resurrection, Appearances and Ascension of Christ 105

Lesson 1

The Sources of the Gospels

Except for scant references by Josephus and Tacitus these four books represent the only information about the Son of God.

Matthew

Viewed in his account, the Jewish perspective.

1. From chapter nine, what do we find as Matthew's occupation? (Matt. 9:9) _____

2. Compare Mark 2:15 and Luke 5:29. _____

Mark

1. List as many facts as you can concerning Mark from the following passages:

   Acts 12:12 _____

   Colossians 4:10 _____

   Acts 15:38 _____

   2 Timothy 4:11 _____

Luke

Luke's style and choice of words/grammar are indicative of his education. He wrote Acts too, much of it in the first person.

1. What is Luke's purpose and method? (Lk. 1:1-4) _____

2. Why does Luke need to rely on "eyewitnesses?" _____
   _____

3. What was Luke's occupation? (Col. 4:14) _____

John

John was present at many of the miracles and was jailed with Peter (Acts 4:19).

1. How is the relationship between Jesus and John described? _____
   _____

2. What was most likely the occupation of John? (Jn. 21:1-3) _____
   _____

Lesson 2

The Pre-Existence, Incarnation and Genealogies of Jesus

Pre-existence and incarnation (Jn. 1:1-14)

1. Who is the Word? Explain. _____
   _____
   _____

2. When was the Word non-existent? (Jn. 17:5) _____
   _____
   _____

3. What does incarnation mean? Contrast John 1:1 and John 1:14. _____
   _____
   _____

4. Who/what became flesh? (1 Tim. 3:16) _____
   _____

5. What role did Jesus have in creation? (Col. 1:16-17, Heb. 1:3, Rev. 19:13) _____
   _____
   _____

6. From John 1:14, what intention did God have by the Word being made flesh? (Heb. 1:3) _____
   _____
   _____

7. Give a "key" phrase or verse in John 1:1-14. _____
   _____
   _____

The genealogies of Jesus

Jesus was established as the seed of Abraham on both sides.

1. Which Gospels list the genealogies of Jesus? _____

   _____

2. What are the two different bloodlines in the these accounts and what is their significance? _____

   _____

   _____

Lesson 3

The Birth of John the Baptist and Jesus and Their Childhood

The announcement of John the Baptist's birth (Lk. 1:5-25)

1. What is revealed about the character of John's parents? (Lk. 1:6, 8) _____

2. What is revealed about John's mission? (Lk 1:16-17) _____

3. What is Zacharias' reaction and what was wrong with it? (Lk. 1:18, 20) _____

4. What's the difference between Zacharias' faith in the angel's message and the faith of an individual today who disbelieves the Word of God (Bible)? _____

5. Why would God use old people to parent John the Baptist? _____

The announcement of Jesus' birth to Mary (Lk. 1:26-38)

1. What are the similarities and differences in the events surrounding the announcements made to Zacharias and Mary? _____

2. What is the age difference between John and Jesus? (Lk. 1:26) _____

_____

3. Concerning Mary's visit to Elizabeth (Lk. 1:39-45), what was Mary's reaction? (Lk. 1:38, 46-55)_____

_____

The announcement of Jesus' birth to Joseph (Matt. 1:18-25)

1. What example can we imitate from Joseph? (Matt. 1:19-24)_____

_____

_____

2. Who named Jesus? Compare Matthew 1:25 with Luke 2:21. _____

_____

The birth and childhood of John the Baptist (Lk. 1:57-80)

1. How did Elizabeth demonstrate a higher regard for the word of the Lord than popular opinion (Lk. 1:59, 60)? Make a personal application. _____

_____

_____

2. After studying Zacharias' prophecy of Luke 1:68-79, list two key phrases or thoughts._____

_____

_____

3. When did John the Baptist begin his spiritual development? _____

_____

The birth of Jesus and other associated events (Lk. 2:1-28)

1. Read Micah 5:2. Explain how men unknowingly participated in the fulfillment of this prophecy. _____

_____

_____

LESSON 3 The Birth of John the Baptist and Jesus and Their Childhood

2. What did the shepherds do with the "good tidings of great joy?" _____
   _____
   _____

3. What economic statement is made by the sacrifice which Mary and Joseph offered? (Lev. 12:8) _____
   _____

4. What does Simeon have his heart set on and what was the basis of his hope?
   _____
   _____

5. What does the "fall and rising of many in Israel" and the other statements Simeon makes to Mary mean in verse 34? Make an application of this today.
   _____
   _____
   _____

6. In one sentence, sum up the character and life of Anna. _____.
   _____
   _____

7. Notice Luke 2:40, then list the verses in our text where Joseph and Mary demonstrate obedience to civil and spiritual laws. _____
   _____
   _____

Wise men from the east visit the Messiah; His flight and return (Matt. 2:1-23)

1. After carefully examining Matthew 2:16, what would be the likely age of Jesus when the wise men arrived to visit? _____

2. Was the star, which led the wise men, merely a natural occurrence? _____
   _____

3. What was the motive behind Herod's treachery? _____
   _____

4. Even though God informed Joseph and Mary about impending troubles and which way to turn, did He physically intervene to protect His son? What can be learned from this? _____
   _____
   _____

5. What 2 purposes does God accomplish by Jesus' flight and return to Nazareth?
   _____
   _____
   _____

The childhood of Jesus (Lk. 2:40-52)

1. Note Luke 2:40. This is the only statement in the Gospels regarding Jesus' childhood from the age of approximately 2 until 12. What is inferred? _____
   _____
   _____

2. What statement from Luke 2:46-50 do you think reveals the extraordinary ability of Jesus? _____
   _____
   _____

3. Why do you suppose the young man Jesus, at the age of 12, understood His responsibilities? Why don't young adults understand their responsibilities? _____
   _____
   _____

John the Baptist, his early message and the messenger (Matt. 3:1-12; Mk. 1:2-8; Lk. 3:2-20)

1. What are some of the characteristics of John's preaching? _____
   _____
   _____

LESSON 3 The Birth of John the Baptist and Jesus and Their Childhood

2. How many miracles did John perform? (Use a concordance and examine the references for the word "miracles" in the four gospels.) _____
   _____

3. What thoughts are inferred after examining the territory where John preached along with his diet and dress? _____
   _____
   _____

4. What role did John play in the coming of Christ? Explain your answer. _____
   _____
   _____

5. What kind of response (numeric) did John's preaching produce? _____
   _____
   _____

6. Would the people he preached to (country folk) have made any difference in the numeric results? (1 Cor. 1:26) _____
   _____

7. What statements or phrases from John's preaching define his "style?" _____
   _____
   _____

8. John exposes one of the rationalisms that gave the Jews a false sense of security. What is it? Make an application to us today. _____
   _____
   _____
   _____

9. What do the figures of speech used in Luke 3:9 mean? _____
   _____
   _____

10. What is the baptism of fire in Luke 3:16 and how does this thought connect with verse 17? _____
_____
_____

Jesus' baptism (Matt. 3:13-17; Mk. 1:9-11; Lk. 3:21-23)

1. Since John's baptism was "of repentance for the remission of sins" (Lk. 3:3), why was Jesus baptized? _____
_____
_____

2. Which law was Jesus exempt from, because of his stature? _____
_____
_____

3. What statement should the fact that Jesus was baptized, make to the person who is skeptical about baptism today? _____
_____
_____

4. What conclusion can be drawn from the events immediately following Jesus' baptism? _____
_____
_____

Lesson 4

The Beginning of Christ's Public Ministry

The temptation of Jesus (Mk. 1:12-13; Matt. 4:1-11; Lk. 4:1-13)

1. What technique(s) does Satan use to tempt Jesus? What other New Testament verses inform us of these "devices?" Make a personal application. _____

2. In Matthew 4:8-9, the first two temptations were to get Jesus to actually exercise His sovereignty over the laws of nature (stones to bread, deliverance by angels), which He could have done. However, the last temptation involves Satan making good on a promise. Do you think he could have done this? If so, how? _____

3. What does Satan reveal about his knowledge in the statements he makes to Jesus? _____

4. What are two important observations from Luke 4:13-14 that we can apply to ourselves? _____

John the Baptist's testimony and encounter with Jesus (Jn. 1:19-34)

1. Who was concerned about John's identity? _____

2. Why would these men ask John if he was Elijah? (Think, use some reference books and see Matthew 11:11.) Harmonize this with Luke 1:17. _____
_____
_____
_____

3. What was John's estimation of himself compared with Christ? _____
_____

4. Which verse reveals John's familiarity with Jesus? _____
_____

5. What evidence does John use to substantiate Jesus as the Lamb of God? _____
_____
_____

The first disciples (Jn. 1:35-51)

1. Of whom does Jesus recruit His first disciple? (Jn. 1:37) _____
_____

2. What are some lessons to learn from Nathanael? (Jn. 1:46) _____
_____

Jesus' first miracle (Jn. 2:1-12)

1. What kind of wine did Jesus make (i.e. intoxicating or other)? Give proof. _____
_____
_____

2. What reasons are given for this miracle? (Jn. 1:11) _____
_____
_____

3. Who are Jesus' traveling companions? (Jn. 1:12) _____
_____
_____

LESSON 4 The Beginning of Christ's Public Ministry

Jesus cleanses the temple (Jn. 2:13-25)

1. Is this the same account of cleansing the temple as found in Matthew 21, Mark 11 and Luke 19? Explain. _____
   _____
   _____

2. What application can we make of John 2:16? _____
   _____
   _____

3. What is Jesus referring to in John 2:19 and 21? _____
   _____
   _____

4. What are some conclusions to be drawn from John 2:23? _____
   _____
   _____

5. What is meant by the writer's comments in John 2:24-25? _____
   _____
   _____

Jesus with Nicodemus (Jn. 3:1-21)

1. Why might Nicodemus have come at night? And what seems to be his initial reaction? (Note: This is mentioned again in John 7:50.) _____
   _____

2. Is there any indication here or in other places that Nicodemus obeyed Christ? _____
   _____

3. In general terms, what is Jesus alluding to with the matter of being "born again," and why does Nicodemus miss the point? _____
   _____
   _____

4. In specific terms, what does "born of water and of the Spirit" mean? List other verses which complement your explanation. _____
_____
_____

5. How does Jesus' statement in verse 8 explain this better? _____
_____
_____

6. What are the "earthly things" that Jesus tells Nicodemus? _____
_____
_____

7. What does John 3:13 reveal about the qualification of Jesus? _____
_____
_____

8. Explain the contrast with Moses, the serpent and Christ. (Also see John 8:28; 12:32-34.) _____
_____
_____

9. Using the context of John 3:14-21, explain away the doctrine of "faith only." _____
_____
_____

Another encounter between Jesus and John the Baptist (Jn. 3:22-36)

1. What question troubles John's disciples? _____
_____
_____

2. Explain John 3:31-33 (especially verse 33). _____
_____
_____

LESSON 4 The Beginning of Christ's Public Ministry

Jesus leaves Judaea and meets the woman at the well (Jn. 4:1-42)

1. Compare verses 1-4 with Mark 1:14; Matthew 4:12; and Luke 4:14. Why does Jesus leave Judaea? (See Matthew 4:12.) _____
   _____
   _____

2. What applications can be learned from the Jesus, "the master personal worker?"
   _____
   _____
   _____

3. What is Jesus referring to in John 4:21-24? _____
   _____
   _____

4. What demonstrates the conviction of this woman? (Jn. 4:28-29) _____
   _____
   _____

5. What point is Jesus trying to make with His disciples in John 4:34-38? _____
   _____
   _____

6. What are some of the characteristics of this woman which could be imitated?
   _____
   _____
   _____

Lesson 5

The Galilean Ministry

The healing at Cana (Jn. 4:43-54)

1. The nobleman seems to have two reasons for inquiring of Jesus. What are they? (Jn. 4:48) _____
_____
_____

2. What fact regarding this miracle removes any doubt as to the possibility that Jesus was a trickster? _____
_____
_____

3. Since the effect of this miracle is recorded, what then was the purpose of it? (Jn. 4:53)
_____
_____

Rejection at Nazareth (Lk. 4:16-30)

1. What is the significance of the passage that Jesus read? _____
_____
_____

2. In your own words, what did Jesus say that enraged them so? _____
_____
_____

3. Jesus made a statement in these verses which tells us why He moved on to Capernaum as found in Matthew 4:13-16. What is it? _____
_____
_____

Four become fishers of men (Matt. 4:18-22; Mk. 1:16-20; Lk. 5:1-11)

1. What is unique about these two pairs of men? _____

2. Luke's account reveals something that the other two accounts omit, what is it, and its significance? _____

3. Why did Peter say what is recorded in Luke 5:8? _____

4. What statement in Luke's account do these four men leave that we could imitate? (Lk. 5:11) _____

The healing of the demoniac in the synagogue (Mk. 1:21-28; Lk. 4:31-37)

1. What is different about Jesus' teaching? _____

2. What does the demon recognize and what passage does he quote? _____

3. What is the reaction to this scene? Had they ever seen this before? _____

LESSON 5 The Galilean Ministry

Jesus heals Peter's mother-in-law and many others (Matt. 8:14-17; Mk. 1:29-34; Lk. 4:38-43)

1. What is revealed in Luke's account that shows us the elapsed time needed for this woman to be healed? _____
   _____
   _____

2. What statement reveals Jesus' purpose and intent? _____
   _____
   _____

Jesus leaves Capernaum and sets out on tour (Matt. 4:23-24; Mk. 1:35-39; Lk. 4:44)

1. Where do the disciples find Jesus before they leave? _____
   _____

2. With whom and where does he go? _____
   _____
   _____

3. What seems to be making the most impact on the people? _____ _____
   _____
   _____

A leper healed (Matt. 8:1-4; Mk. 1:40-45; Lk. 5:12-16)

1. Of what is the leper sure? _____
   _____
   _____

2. Besides the fact that Jesus was trying to keep a low profile, what may be another reason that He told the leper to "tell no man?" _____
   _____
   _____

3. Why is the leper instructed to "offer a gift?" (Lev. 14:1-32) Application? _____
   _____
   _____

4. From the impact of the leper's testimony to the public, how can we be sure this was a "genuine" miracle? _____
   _____
   _____

The healing of a paralytic (Matt. 9:1-8; Mk. 2:1-12; Lk. 5:17-26)

1. What is Jesus' purpose for this gathering? _____
   _____
   _____

2. Jesus "saw their faith." What demonstrated such? Make an application or offer a complementary verse._____
   _____
   _____

3. What does the statement, "Son, thy sins are forgiven thee," have to do with his healing?   Is he a paralytic because of his sins?_____
   _____
   _____

4. In your own words, express Jesus' reasoning in Mark 2:8-11. _____
   _____
   _____

The calling of Matthew (Matt. 9:9-13; Mk. 2:13-17; Lk. 5:27-32)

1. Luke's account records a statement revealing Matthew's determination, what is it?
   _____
   _____

2. What are the scribes and Pharisees trying to do to Jesus with their indictment, and what application can we make from Jesus' reply? _____

Disciples defended via a parable (Matt. 9:14-17; Mk. 2:18-22; Lk. 5:33-39)

1. Jesus responds in three parables to this question. What is He really talking about?

Healing on the Sabbath and Jesus' defense about it (Jn. 5:1-47)

1. What charges are brought by the Jews? _____

2. Does the crippled man know who Jesus is or who healed him? Explain. Notice the Jews did not dispute the validity of this miracle. _____

3. What evidence does Jesus use in His defense of these groundless charges? _____

4. What statements does Jesus make that show He is indeed equal with God? _____

5. List what you think are other significant points from Jesus' statements in John 5:28-29 and John 42-47. Explain. _____

A second Sabbath controversy (Matt. 12:1-8; Mk. 2:23-28; Lk. 6:1-5)

1. Did the disciples do anything wrong? Explain. _____
   _____
   _____

2. What are some points from these three accounts that one must study to have the complete story? _____
   _____
   _____

3. What is the significance of the statement "the Son of man is lord even of the Sabbath?" _____
   _____
   _____

A third Sabbath controversy and healing (Matt. 12:9-14; Mk. 3:1-6; Lk. 6:6-11)

1. Which hand was withered? _____

2. In your own words, what word best describes the motive of the bystanders? ____
   _____

3. What method does Jesus use to head off their thinking? Make an application. ____
   _____
   _____
   _____

4. What do the Pharisees determine to do? Explain how people react today in a similar fashion when confronted with the truth. _____
   _____
   _____

Jesus teaches and heals by the Sea of Galilee (Matt. 12:15-21; Mk. 3:7-12)

1. Why did Jesus withdraw to the sea? _____
   _____
   _____

2. In your own words, make list of the characteristics of Jesus from Isaiah's prophecy as Matthew 12:18-21 records them and explain. Examine Mark's account. _____
   _____
   _____

Jesus selects the twelve (Lk. 6:12-16; Mk. 3:13-19)

1. What reason is given for selecting these men? _____
   _____
   _____

2. List the names of the apostles and then list as many prominent New Testament men as you can who are not among this list. _____
   _____
   _____
   _____
   _____

The sermon on the mount (Matt. 5-7 and Lk. 6:12-16): introduction and the beatitudes (Matt. 5:1-12)

1. To what class of people are the beatitudes addressed? _____
   _____

2. Each beatitude contrasts an attitude or disposition with a reward. Explain this principle. (Rom. 11:22) _____
   _____

Influence (Matt. 5:13-16)

1. Explain characteristics of light and salt that define influence. _____
   _____
   _____

The teaching of the Law contrasted with popular views (Matt. 5:17-48)

1. Jesus contrasts popular notions about the law with the truth of the law in six different categories. What are they, and who has been responsible for the perversions? (Matt. 5:20) _____
   _____
   _____
   _____

2. What does Jesus mean by the statement in Matthew 5:17-18? (Also see Galatians 3:19-21.) _____
   _____
   _____

3. What was the major flaw in the "righteousness of the scribes and Pharisees?" (Also see Romans 2:28.) _____
   _____
   _____

4. How was the command stated in Matthew 5:21 being perverted? Make an application. _____
   _____
   _____

5. What is the real spiritual truth Jesus is teaching in Matthew 5:21-26? _____
   _____
   _____

LESSON 5 The Galilean Ministry

6. How was the command in Matthew 5:27 being perverted? _____
   _____
   _____

7. What is the real spiritual truth Jesus is teaching in Matthew 5:29-30? _____
   _____
   _____

8. How was the command in Matthew 5:31 being perverted, and what was the real truth as presented by Jesus? _____
   _____
   _____

9. Explain what is the issue in Matthew 5:33-37? Why does Jesus mention this? _____
   _____
   _____

10. In Matthew 5:38-42, Jesus sets forth four examples of how a person should submit rather than retaliate. Explain each one. _____
    _____
    _____
    _____
    _____

11. Since the scribes and the Pharisees misused the application of the Law of Moses about "an eye for an eye," etc., what is the correct application? _____
    _____
    _____

12. Where does the Bible say "love your enemies and hate thy neighbor?" _____
    _____
    _____

13. Give an application of each of the four commands of Matthew 5:44. _____

    _____
    _____
    _____

14. From the text, what reason is given for keeping the commandments of Matthew 5:44 and what example is given as evidence? _____

    _____
    _____
    _____

Jesus teaches of real righteousness (Matt. 6:1-18)

1. What three works of righteousness are mentioned in this text, and how are they to be implemented? _____

    _____
    _____
    _____

2. In your own words, explain Matthew 6:1-5, and give good and bad examples. ____

    _____
    _____
    _____

3. Jesus addresses the matter of prayer in Matthew 6:5-15. What does He mean by "they have their reward?" _____

    _____
    _____

4. What are "vain repetitions?" Can you think of a New Testament example of such?

    _____
    _____

LESSON 5 The Galilean Ministry 31

5. What are the basic elements of the model prayer in Matthew 6:9-15? _____
   _____
   _____
   _____

6. From Matthew 6:16-18, what is hypocritical about the fasting that Jesus observed?
   _____

Jesus teaches of life's cares and riches (Matt. 6:19-34)

1. In your own words, what is the contrast made in Matthew 6:19-21?_____
   _____
   _____

2. Is it wrong to "lay up" money or securities for the future (i.e. retirement)? Explain.
   _____
   _____

3. Explain the verses in Matthew 6:22-23 and how they contextually fit into this discourse about riches. _____
   _____
   _____

4. Make an application of Matthew 6:24. _____
   _____
   _____

5. In what way are we not to worry about life's necessities? (Matt. 6:25)_____
   _____
   _____

6. What is the significance of the comparison with Solomon in Matthew 6:29?_____
   _____
   _____

7. What is the meaning of the comparison to the statement in Matthew 6:32 where the Lord said, "for after these things do the Gentiles seek?" _____
_____
_____

Judging and prudence (Matt. 7:1-6)

1. What type of judgment is Jesus condemning? _____
_____
_____

2. How will you be judged? _____
_____

3. What are the first two concerns one should have when passing judgment? _____
_____
_____

4. What purpose do the two illustrations of Matthew 7:6 serve? Give an example.
_____
_____
_____

Prayer (Matt. 7:7-12)

1. "Ask" and "seek" as commanded by Jesus on contingencies for what? _____
_____
_____

2. What will the Father give to them that ask? _____
_____
_____

3. How does Matthew 7:12 (which begins with the word "therefore") fit into the context of Matthew 7:7-11? _____
_____

LESSON 5 The Galilean Ministry

The sermon concluded with powerful parables (Matt. 7:13-29)

1. List as many contrasts as you can in Matthew 7:13-29 (i.e. wide and narrow). _____

2. In your own words, what is the spiritual truth Jesus is making in these parables?

3. In Matthew 7:14, is Jesus saying "the way" is obscure, and the reason people do not find it?

4. What does "know them by their fruits" mean concerning the false prophets? (2 Pet. 2)

5. Who do you think Matthew 7:21 is describing and why? _____

6. What might the rains, floods, and wind be representing in Matthew 7:24-27? _____

7. What contrast is used to describe Jesus' "sermon on the mount?" (Matt. 7:29) _____

The centurion's servant is healed (Matt. 8:5-13; Lk. 7:1-10)

1. How is the relationship between the centurion and his servant described? What word(s) describes the centurion's character? Make spiritual application of these observations. (Lk. 7:2) _____

2. What does the centurion apparently know about Jesus? Explain. (Lk. 7:7) _____
   _____
   _____

3. What is the significance of Jesus' statement in Matthew 8:10: "I have not found so great faith, no, not in Israel?" What do the following statements in Matthew 8:11-12 signify?
   _____
   _____
   _____

The widow's son at Nain is raised (Lk. 7:11-17)

1. What are two purposes for Jesus performing this miracle, though not specifically stated? _____
   _____
   _____

John the Baptist's inquiry and Jesus' estimation of John (Matt. 11:2-19; Lk. 7:18-35)

1. Where is John and of what does he seem uncertain? _____
   _____
   _____

2. How does Jesus answer John's question? _____
   _____
   _____

3. Is Jesus minimizing John the Baptist with statements like "a reed shaken with the wind" and "a man clothed in soft raiment?" _____
   _____

4. How was John "more than a prophet?" (Matt. 11:9) _____
   _____
   _____

LESSON 5 The Galilean Ministry

5. How could John be as great as any born of woman, and be less than the least in the kingdom of heaven? _____

6. What does Jesus reveal about the reception of John's ministry in Matthew 11:12? _____

7. Compare Acts 7:52 to question 6 and comment. _____

8. In your own words, what is Jesus' estimation of "this generation?" _____

9. What does Matthew 11:18-19 reveal about the world's attitude toward what is good? _____

Woes pronounced upon the cities (Matt. 11:20-30)

1. What is wrong with the cities Jesus upbraided? _____

2. Why will it be more tolerable in the day of judgment for Tyre, Sidon, and Sodom than these cities? _____

The anointing of Christ's feet and the parable of the two debtors (Lk. 7:36-50)

1. What is the irony of the Pharisee's thoughts in Luke 7:39 and Jesus' response? _____

2. Jesus is talking about the value of forgiveness. How can we make an application of this today? _____

3. It seems as though only one point clearly "stuck" on the minds of the bystanders. What was it? _____

Accusations against Jesus concerning Beelzebub (Matt. 12:22-37; Mk. 3:19-30)

1. Who is Beelzebub? _____

2. How does Jesus overthrow their faulty reasoning? _____

3. From Mark 3:28-30, explain the fundamental truth Jesus is teaching. _____

4. What exactly is, or how does one blaspheme the Holy Spirit? _____

The scribes and Pharisees demand a sign (Matt. 12:38-45)

1. Why does Jesus rebuke this demand of the scribes and Pharisees? Can you think of a application of this today? _____
   _____
   _____

2. Explain the significance of the contrasts in Matthew 12:40-42.
   _____
   _____
   _____

3. What is Jesus teaching in Matthew 12:43-45? _____
   _____
   _____

Jesus' family requests to see Him (Matt. 12:46-50; Mk. 3:31-35; Lk. 8:19-21)

1. What lesson is Jesus teaching when he responds to the messengers? Make an application. _____
   _____
   _____

The Master begins with the first group of parables: the parable of the sower and soils (Matt. 13:1-23; Mk. 4:1-25; Lk. 8:5-18)

1. List at least five points that can be learned and applied from this parable, though not specifically stated. _____
   _____
   _____
   _____
   _____

2. Explain Mark 4:11-12. Does Jesus discriminate with the understanding of His word?

3. What is the connection between the people of Isaiah's day and these people? _____

4. What were they seeing that earlier prophets and righteous men had looked searched for but not seen? (1 Pet.1:10) _____

Parable of the seed growing (Mk. 4:26-29)

1. What are some spiritual applications of this natural truth? _____

Parable of the tares (Matt. 13:24-30, 36-43)

1. From this parable, who is the man, what is the good seed, and what are the tares?

2. What are some things to be understood from this parable? _____

Parable of the mustard seed (Matt. 13:31-32; Mk. 4:30-32)

1. Explain the spiritual meaning of this parable and make application. _____

Parable of the leaven (Matt. 13:33)

1. What is Jesus teaching in this one verse parable? _____

Parables of the hidden treasure and the pearl of great price (Matt. 13:44-46)

1. What is the fundamental truth Jesus teaches here in these two parables? _____

Parable of the net (Matt. 13:47-50)

1. List as many spiritual observations as possible from this parable. _____

Parable of the householder (Matt. 13:51-53)

1. What spiritual truth is learned from this parable? _____

The stilling of the tempest (Matt. 8:18, 23-27; Mk. 4:35-41; Lk. 8:22-25)

1. How bad was this storm? _____

2. What does the question, "Master, do you not care that we perish?" reveal about the disciples? _____

3. One fear gave way to another. What was it? Explain. _____
_____
_____

Jesus heals a demoniac (Matt. 8:28-34; Mk. 5:1-20; Lk. 8:26-39)

1. How many demoniacs are there? _____

2. What do the demons know about Jesus? _____

3. What request do the bystanders make of Jesus? _____
_____

4. What does the restored man want and what does Jesus say? _____
_____
_____

The healing of Jairus' daughter and the woman who touched Jesus' garment (Matt. 9:18-26; Mk. 5:21-43; Lk. 8:40-56)

1. List some of the "reactions" of different people in these miracles. _____
_____
_____

Jesus heals two blind men and a dumb demoniac (Matt. 9:27-34)

1. What is an ironic thing about the faith of the blind men when contrasted with the faith of others who had faith which enabled them to be healed? _____
_____

2. What is most likely the deep-seated problem of the Pharisees? _____
_____

Jesus' last visit to Nazareth (Matt. 13:54-58; Mk. 6:1-6)

1. What was the attitude toward Jesus on His previous visit home, and has it changed? _____
_____

2. What are the people from Jesus' hometown having a hard time reconciling in their minds? _____

3. Why could Jesus "do no mighty work" here? _____
_____
_____

The third tour of Galilee and the limited commission
(Matt. 9:35-11:1; Mk. 6:6-13; Lk. 9:1-6)

1. What moved Jesus with compassion and what die He tell His disciples? Make an application. _____
_____
_____
_____

2. Where are the 12 disciples to focus their preaching efforts? _____
_____

3. What is Jesus reinforcing in Mark 10:9-10? _____
_____

4. What does Jesus' statement in Matthew 10:16 mean? _____
_____

5. From Matthew 10:17-23, list the things that await these men on this journey. _____
_____
_____

6. How is Jesus trying to comfort these men with the statements in Matthew 10:24-31? _____
_____

7. How does Jesus describe, to these men, the two reactions they will experience with their preaching? _____

8. What is the point Jesus is emphasizing in Matthew 10:34-39? _____

9. How can applications of Mathew 10:40-42 be made to us today? _____

Jesus, John the Baptist and Herod (Matt. 14:1-12; Mk. 6:14-29; Lk. 9:7-9)

1. Herod has two fears: what are they, and what is his estimation of John? _____

2. Why does Herod have John executed, and what statement reflects his conscience? _____

3. What statement infuriates Herodias? Make an application today. _____

4. What word does the Bible use to describe the relationship between Herod and Herodias? _____

The disciples return and retire with Jesus to a desert place and the feeding of 5,000 (Matt. 14:13-21; Mk. 6:30-44; Lk. 9:10-17; Jn. 6:1-13)

1. This is one of four withdrawals Jesus makes. What are some stated reasons and perhaps others for this retreat? _____

LESSON 5 The Galilean Ministry

2. What motivates Jesus to feed the multitude? _____

3. What is Jesus doing when he asked Philip the question? _____

4. What lesson did the 12 learn from this miracle and can we make an application?

Jesus prevents a political uprising and another peril on the water to Gennesaret (Matt. 14:22-36; Mk. 6:45-56; Jn. 6:14-21)

1. Why is the word "constrained" (KJV) used in the matter of departure by boat?

2. List the order of events in the boat. _____

3. What seems to be Peter's purpose in asking, "If it be you...?" _____

4. What kind of reception do they find at Gennesaret? _____

Return to Capernaum (Jn. 6:22-7:1)

1. Those seeking a handout are from where, and what spiritual truth does Jesus teach, being given this opportunity? _____
   _____

2. What are the people challenging Jesus for in John 6:28-34? _____
   _____

3. In your own words, sum up John 6:35-40. _____
   _____
   _____

4. What is used as an excuse for their disbelief? _____
   _____

5. How are people drawn to God? _____
   _____

6. What is the purpose of the contrast in John 6:48-51? _____
   _____

7. What point are the Jews missing in John 6:52? What is the "flesh" and "blood" Jesus refers to in John 6:53-58? (Use other verses to explain your answer.) _____
   _____
   _____
   _____

8. What is the disciples' reaction and how does Jesus clarify the matter for them?
   _____
   _____

Pharisees come from Jerusalem to reproach Jesus (Matt. 15:1-20; Mk. 7:1-23; Jn. 7:1)

1. Why does Jesus leave Judea? _____
   _____

2. What is the problem the Pharisees have with Jesus' disciples and how does Jesus answer? _____
_____
_____

3. What are three things Jesus says is wrong with the commandments and doctrines of men? Make application. _____
_____
_____

4. What tradition does Jesus expose in Mark 7:9-13? _____
_____
_____

5. In Mark 7:14-23 Jesus addresses the real problem. What is it?_____
_____
_____

6. What do the disciples recognize about the content of this message, and how does Jesus react? Make an application. _____
_____
_____
_____

7. List a "key" statement or thought in this dialogue. _____
_____
_____

The second withdrawal to Tyre and Sidon (Matt. 15:21-28; Mk. 7:24-30)

1. What was the reaction to Jesus' last visit to this region? _____
_____

2. What is the advice of the disciples regarding the Canaanite woman? _____
_____

3. What do you think Jesus was doing when he answered the woman's request? _____
   _____

4. Why did Jesus admire this woman's faith? _____
   _____

The third withdrawal and miracles (Matt. 15:29-38; Mk. 7:31-8:9)

1. What might be the explanation for Jesus' actions in Mark 33-34 when healing the deaf man? _____
   _____

2. What does Mark 8:2 say about the motive of this multitude? _____
   _____

3. Do you think there is any significance that Jesus fed them after teaching them?
   _____

A brief visit to Dalmanutha and sharp opposition (Matt. 15:39-16:4; Mk. 8:10-12)

1. What do the religious leaders want to see? How does Jesus respond? _____
   _____
   _____

The fourth withdrawal to Bethsaida (Matt. 16:5-12; Mk. 8:13-26)

1. Why does Jesus rebuke the disciples? _____
   _____

At Caesarea Philippi, Jesus asks the question of who he is (Matt. 16:13-20; Mk. 8:27-30; Lk. 9:18-21)

1. Why do you think the disciples told Jesus of the opinions of others? _____
   _____

2. What does Jesus' statement about "flesh and blood" indicate? _____
   _____
   _____

3. What is the "rock" the church would be built upon? _____

4. What is meant by the statement, "the gates of hell shall not prevail against it?" ___
   _____
   _____

5. What is the "key" of the kingdom? _____

6. What statement places this in a time frame for fulfillment? _____
   _____

7. Why does Jesus make such a statement in Matthew 16:20? _____
   _____
   _____

Jesus prophesizes about His death (Matt. 16:21-26; Mk. 8:31-37; Lk. 9:22-25)

1. Who would be behind the death of Jesus? _____

2. How does Peter demonstrate his impetuous character and how does Jesus respond?
   _____
   _____

3. What is Jesus saying in Matthew 16:24-25? _____
   _____
   _____

4. List thoughts or implications from Matthew 16:25-26 as you can. _____
   _____
   _____

The coming of the kingdom (Matt. 16:27-28; Mk. 8:38-9:1; Lk. 9:26-27)

1. What events regarding the coming of the kingdom would cause people to be ashamed of Jesus? Are there applications to be made today? _____
   _____

2. Jesus and His _____ are inseparable. Explain. _____
   _____
   _____

3. What is the time frame of the kingdom's appearance? _____
   _____

The transfiguration (Matt. 17:1-13; Mk. 9:2-13; Lk. 9:28-36)

1. How many days expired between the episode about the kingdom and the transfiguration? _____

2. What does the "transfiguration" mean? _____
   _____

3. What is the stated purpose for going to the mountain and what is done by the disciples? _____
   _____

4. What do you think is the significance of Moses' and Elijah's appearance, and what was the topic of discussion? _____
   _____
   _____

5. What is Peter's plan, and what do Mark and Luke say about his statement? Explain.
   _____
   _____

6. What is the significance of the Father's reply? _____
   _____

7. When is this event to be revealed to others? _____

8. In view of this event, why do you think the disciples ask, "Why do the scribes say that Elijah must come first?" _____
   _____

9. What was their misconception, and how does Jesus clarify it for them? _____

A demoniac boy healed (Matt. 17:14-20; Mk. 9:14-29; Lk. 9:37-43)

1. Which disciples were unsuccessful in casting out this demon? Explain. _____

2. Why do you suppose the disciples did not have enough faith to relieve this boy? _____

3. How does Jesus answer their question regarding their inability? _____

Jesus again foretells of His death (Matt. 17:22-23; Mk. 9:30-32; Lk. 9:43-45)

1. After reading these accounts, summarize the reasoning and feelings of the disciples. _____

Jesus pays the half-shekel (Matt. 17:24-27)

1. What is the origin of this "half-shekel" tribute and who was asking? _____

2. What is Jesus teaching with these questions He sets before Peter and how does the miracle further substantiate it? _____

The contention over who shall be the greatest and offenses
(Matt. 18:1-14; Mk. 9:33-50; Lk. 9:46-50)

1. What might be causing the disciples to think about this matter? _____
   _____

2. Harmonize the apparent contradiction in Mark 9:33-34 and Luke 9:46 with Matthew 18:1. _____
   _____
   _____

3. How does the illustration with the small child deal with this matter? What does "become as little children" mean? _____
   _____
   _____

4. What is the connection between the illustration with the child and John's statement? _____
   _____
   _____

5. What are the consequences of causing another to stumble? Make an application.
   _____
   _____
   _____

6. In view of Matthew's statement in 18:7 ("but woe to the man through whom the occasion cometh"), what might be the eyes, hands or feet that will cause offenses?
   _____
   _____

7. Is Matthew 18:10 teaching that there are guardian angels? If not, explain. _____
   _____
   _____

LESSON 5 The Galilean Ministry

8. What points can be drawn from Matthew 18:12-14? _____
_____
_____

Our duty and treatment to a brother who has sinned (Matt.18:15-20)

1. Give the scriptural order of restoring the erring. _____
_____

2. What kind of "witnesses" should be utilized in this process? _____
_____

3. What is the "church" in Matthew 18:17? _____
_____

4. What does "let him be as a heathen and publican" mean? _____
_____

5. What should your treatment of this person be, if the church must take disciplinary action? _____
_____
_____

6. What are some unscriptural scenarios that you may have observed? _____
_____
_____
_____

7. How do you explain Matthew 18:18-20 in this setting? _____
_____
_____

Jesus further teaches forgiveness (Matt. 18:21-35)

1. What does the statement "seven times seventy" mean? _____
_____

2. Who are the characters in this parable? _____
   _____

3. What kind of forgiveness does God recognize? _____
   _____

The cost of discipleship (Matt. 8:19-22; Lk. 9:57-62)

1. What is Jesus saying in Matthew 8:20? _____
   _____
   _____

2. In your own words explain Luke 9:62. _____
   _____
   _____

Jesus is asked to go to Judea (Jn. 7:2-9)

1. Who is asking Jesus to go, and what is their disposition? _____
   _____
   _____

2. Why were they asking Jesus to go to Judea and why doesn't He go? ___
   _____
   _____

3. Explain John 7:6. _____
   _____
   _____

Jesus secretly goes to Jerusalem (Lk. 9:51-56; Jn. 7:10)

1. What is meant by the phrase "when the days were well-nigh come that he should be received up?" _____
   _____
   _____

LESSON 6 The Judean Ministry

2. Why does Jesus send messengers ahead? _____
_____
_____

3. What do James and John propose, and how does Jesus react? _____
_____
_____

Lesson 6

The Judean Ministry

Jesus goes to the feast of tabernacles (Jn. 7:11-52)

1. Explain the Jews' attitude, apprehensions, and preconceived thoughts. _____

2. Of what does Jesus indict them? _____

3. What was some of the Jews' hypocrisy that Jesus exposes? _____

4. What kind of judgment is Jesus condemning? _____

5. What do some reason in John 7:25-28, and how does Jesus respond? _____

6. What question shows the difficulty some believers were still having? _____

7. How are the Pharisees confused by Jesus' statements in John 7:33-34? _____

8. What verse does Jesus quote that seems to change the mind of some? _____

9. What answer is given for not apprehending Jesus?_____
   _____

10. Summarize the conclusion from John 7:47-53. _____
    _____
    _____

The adulteress brought to Jesus (Jn. 7:53-8:11)

1. What was the motive of the men who brought this woman to Jesus? _____
   _____
   _____

2. Should Jesus' response to these charges be construed to mean that punishment according to the Law of Moses was not to be inflicted? Explain._____
   _____
   _____

More anger of the Pharisees as they are exposed (Jn. 8:12-59)

1. What is the charge of the Pharisees and how does Jesus counter?_____
   _____
   _____

2. What does Jesus mean by the statement in John 8:19? _____
   _____
   _____

3. What underlying thought is Jesus expressing in John 8:21-30 and what is the reaction? _____
   _____
   _____

4. In the context of this study, what does John 8:31-32 say about Jesus' judgment of their situation? _____
   _____

LESSON 6 The Judean Ministry   57

5. What does John 8:33 (which is a response to verses 31-32) demonstrate about the believing Jews? Make an application. _____
_____
_____

6. Jesus further explains their situation in John 8:34-38. How does this illustration serve in teaching this? _____
_____
_____

7. From John 8:39 and 41, how are Jesus' statements understood? _____
_____
_____

8. What does Jesus mean by "ye cannot hear my word" in John 8:43? _____
_____
_____

9. What are these men doing that make them live up to the charge in John 8:44?
_____
_____

10. When cornered with the truth, many times people resort to other tactics. What do the Jews do at this point? _____
_____

11. In John 8:54, how has Christ previously shown the Jews that He has honored the Father? _____
_____

12. Explain the following statements about the relationship between Christ and Abraham:

   a. "Abraham rejoiced to see my day and he saw it" _____

_____

  b. "before Abraham was, I am." _____

_____

Jesus heals a blind man who outwits the Pharisees (Jn. 9:1-41)

1. What do the disciples think is the problem with this man? What are some other verses that overthrow this reasoning? _____

_____

_____

2. What happens between the time the man is healed and is taken to the Pharisees?

_____

_____

3. How do the Pharisees react? _____

_____

_____

4. How do the parents respond when asked about this situation, and why? ____

_____

_____

5. What do the Jews try this time when asking the man? What is his response, and what results from the stand he takes? _____

_____

_____

6. What are some points to be learned from John 9:35-38? _____

_____

_____

7. What is the point of Jesus' teaching in John 9:39-41? _____

_____

_____

LESSON 6 The Judean Ministry   59

The parable of the good shepherd and the sheep (Jn. 10:1-21)

1. Jesus set forth this parable to the Pharisees, which they did not understand. Who are the characters in the parable, and what is the parable's point? _____
   _____
   _____

2. What are the reactions? _____
   _____
   _____

The mission of the seventy and their return (Lk. 10:1-24)

1. What is to be the "mission" of this mission? _____
   _____

2. Why might the Lord have set forth the stipulations in Luke 10:3-4? _____
   _____
   _____

3. What does the "son of peace" in Luke 10:6 mean? _____
   _____
   _____

4. Explain Luke 10:10-11. _____
   _____
   _____

5. In your own words, summarize Luke 10:12-16. _____
   _____
   _____

6. What does the report of the seventy to Jesus indicate, and how does he respond?
   _____
   _____

7. Jesus seems to have reached a significant milestone as revealed in Luke 10:21-24. Explain. _____
   _____
   _____

Jesus answers a lawyer's question with a parable (Lk. 10:25-37)

1. What is the lawyer trying to do with his question? _____
   _____
   _____

2. Before reading the parable, what can one conclude from Luke 10:29 to be the lawyer's problem? _____
   _____

3. Why do you think Jesus identifies the characters in this parable so specifically (i.e. priest, Levite, Samaritan)? _____
   _____
   _____

4. List as many points from this parable as possible. _____
   _____
   _____
   _____

Jesus goes to Martha's house (Lk. 10:38-42)

1. Martha and Mary represent two classes of people. What/who are they? _____
   _____
   _____

2. What does Jesus' statement in Luke 10:41 teach us today? _____
   _____
   _____

LESSON 6 The Judean Ministry

Jesus again gives a model prayer (Lk. 11:1-13)

1. The disciples say to Jesus, "Teach us to pray," but Jesus seems to deal with a different aspect of prayer. What is it? _____
   _____

2. How do the figures Jesus uses in this parable help one understand the problem associated have with prayer? _____
   _____

Jesus is accused of being in league with Beelzebub (Lk. 11:14-36)

1. What is Jesus' response to the charge that He is in agreement with Beelzebub?
   _____
   _____

2. In the context of this setting, explain the parable in Luke 11:21-26. _____
   _____
   _____

3. From Luke 11:27-28, what can one conclude about the veneration of Mary, the mother of Jesus? _____
   _____

4. Why does Jesus consider the people an "evil generation" for seeking a sign? _____
   _____
   _____

5. What is the sign of Jonas? _____
   _____

6. In what sense does the "queen of the south" and the "men of Nineveh" condemn the generation that Jesus was addressing? _____
   _____
   _____

7. In what way is Luke 11:33-36 connected to previous statements of Jesus in this discourse? _____
_____
_____

Jesus denounces the Pharisees and lawyers and excites their anger (Lk. 11:37-54)

1. After considering these verses, what might have been the motive of the Pharisee who invited Jesus to dine? _____
_____

2. From Luke 11:39-44, list the things that Jesus indicts the Pharisees of and how these charges are made peculiar to this class of Jews? _____
_____
_____
_____

3. From Luke 11:46-52, list the things that Jesus indicts the lawyers of and how these charges are made peculiar to this class of Jews? _____
_____
_____
_____

4. What is the reaction to the plain truth of Jesus? _____
_____
_____

Jesus speaks to a vast crowd in parables about many topics (Lk. 12:1-59)

1. In your own words, list the major points from Luke 12:1-12. _____
_____
_____
_____

LESSON 6 The Judean Ministry   63

2. From Luke 12:1 where it says he spoke to "disciples first," what things mentioned in Luke 12:1-12 would be peculiar to those disciples? What is the reason for Jesus saying these things? _____
   _____
   _____

3. What does the question in Luke 12:13 reveal about the character of the petitioner?
   _____
   _____

4. In Luke 12:16-19, on whom is the rich fool focused? _____
   _____

5. What is wrong with riches? _____
   _____

6. What is the major premise Jesus is setting forth in Luke 12:22-34? _____
   _____
   _____

7. What statement of Jesus from Luke 12:22-34 do you believe reveals an element of danger? _____
   _____

8. List each thing (like the raven) that Jesus uses to illustrate this premise and write a one-sentence statement that teaches this. _____
   _____
   _____
   _____

9. List one word that sums up Luke 12:35-40 and explain. _____
   _____
   _____

10. How does the parable in Luke 12:42-48 answer Peter's question in Luke 12:41?
    _____
    _____

11. What principle does Luke 12:48 teach, and what other parable does this resemble?
    _____
    _____

12. What do you think the fire of Luke 12:49 is and why? _____
    _____
    _____

13. What is the "baptism" of Luke 12:50? _____
    _____

14. What is the point of Luke 12:49-53?_____
    _____
    _____

15. How can we harmonize Luke 12:49-53 with John 14:27 and 16:33?_____
    _____
    _____

16. What is Jesus teaching in Luke 12:54-57? _____
    _____
    _____

17. What does Jesus mean by "this time" in Luke 12:56? _____
    _____
    _____

18. How does Luke 12:58-59 serve as a summary to the things that Jesus has just said?
    _____
    _____

Repentance demanded of all (Lk. 13:1-9)

1. What are the informers of Luke 13:1 trying to do? _____

2. What purpose does Jesus' two illustrations serve to teach? _____

Jesus heals a crippled woman and repeats parables of the mustard seed and leaven (Lk. 13:10-22)

1. How is Jesus misrepresented? Make an application today. _____

2. How does Jesus expose this charge, and what are the reactions? _____

3. What overall theme or thought do the two parables in Luke 13:18-21 teach? _____

The Feast of Dedication, an attempt to stone Jesus and another reference to John the Baptist (Jn. 10:22-42)

1. What do the Jews ask Jesus, and in your own words how does He respond? _____

2. What is it about Jesus' statements that provoke them to stone Him? _____

3. Where is the quotation located from the law Jesus mentions in John 10:34, and what is His reasoning from it? _____
_____
_____

4. Compare John 10:41 and Luke 1:15. What is a significant point to be learned when making this comparison? _____
_____
_____

Lesson 7

The Perean Ministry

Who is saved? And a warning to flee Herod (Lk. 13:23-35)

1. What is the answer to the question of Luke 13:23? _____
   _____
   _____

2. Jesus said seekers have a time limitation on entering the kingdom. What is it?
   _____
   _____

3. Who are the people of Luke 13:26? _____
   _____

4. What points can be learned from Luke 13:28-30 about the unseen eternity that awaits? _____
   _____
   _____

5. What does the prediction of Jesus to Herod in Luke 13:32-33 say to Herod? _____
   _____

6. What has been the Jews' attitude towards prophets, and what NT preacher made a similar statement? _____
   _____
   _____

7. Explain Luke 13:35. _____
   _____
   _____

Dining with a chief Pharisee, healing on the Sabbath, and three parables (Lk. 14:1-24)

1. Jesus has a different approach before healing on the Sabbath. What is it? _____

2. What is the lesson of Luke 14:8-11? _____

3. What might the parable in Luke 14:12-14 be saying about the motive of the chief Pharisee where Jesus is eating? _____

4. Jesus' parable in Luke 14:16-24 teaches several things. What are they, and considering his audience, what is the special significance to them? _____

Great crowds and the cost of discipleship (Lk. 14:25-35)

1. What principle is taught in Luke 14:26-27? _____

2. Is Luke 14:28-31 teaching that not everyone has the wherewithal to be a disciple? Explain your answer._____

Jesus receives sinners and defends Himself with three parables (Lk. 15:1-32)

1. What is Jesus motive for "receiving sinners?" What is lacking in those making this accusation? _____

2. Make some practical applications from Luke 15:4-10. _____

3. From Luke 15:11-32, who does the younger son represent? _____

4. What statement(s) from Luke 15:11-17 show a turning point in the son's life? _____

5. Luke 15:17-18 demonstrates another characteristic of this son to be imitated. What is It? _____

6. What statement shows that this man did not go home because of personal need? _____

7. Of whom is the father's behavior indicative? _____

8. Who does the older son represent? _____

9. What does the statement in Luke 15:31 show? _____

10. What are some practical lessons can be learned and applied from this story? _____
_____
_____

The unjust or unrighteous steward (Lk. 16:1-13)

1. What is the steward's plan after being confronted with mishandling the rich man's affairs? _____
_____
_____

2. Why is the steward "commended" by his master for further fraudulence? And, explain the latter half of Luke 16:8. _____
_____
_____
_____

3. Explain Jesus' statement in Luke 16:9. _____
_____
_____

4. What is the point of Jesus' summary in Luke 16:10-13?_____
_____
_____

Jesus confronts the Pharisees and uses the story of the rich man and Lazarus to further condemn them (Lk.16:14-18)

1. Besides being covetous, what is the other problem Jesus exposes for the Pharisees? _____
_____

2. Explain Luke 16:16-17. _____
_____
_____

LESSON 7 The Perean Ministry

3. Why do you think Jesus introduces the subject of Luke 16:18 in this dialogue? _____
   _____
   _____

4. How does the story in Luke 16:19-31 connect with the preceding thoughts? _____
   _____
   _____

5. What are the rich man's two biggest problems? _____
   _____
   _____

6. What are the common things that the rich man and Lazarus share? _____
   _____
   _____

7. What are the contrasts made by Abraham? _____
   _____
   _____

8. What are requests of the rich man? Lazarus? _____
   _____
   _____

9. Who or what is Abraham referring to in Luke 16:29? _____
   _____

10. Jesus is telling this story, what is the irony to be found in Luke 16:31? _____
    _____

11. This story provides scriptural proof to overthrow several false doctrines. What are they? _____
    _____
    _____

Jesus raises Lazarus from the dead, and its effect (Jn. 11:1-54)

1. How is the relationship between Jesus and the family of Lazarus described, and why? _____

   _____

   _____

2. Jesus states the reason for this sickness and miracle at least three times in the text. Identify them and explain. _____

   _____

   _____

   _____

3. What are the disciples concerned with, and what is Jesus reply? _____

   _____

   _____

4. What does Jesus do before arriving that demonstrates an attribute of deity? _____

   _____

   _____

5. What is the meaning of Thomas' statement in John 11:16? _____

   _____

   _____

6. Perhaps Martha has experienced some spiritual development. Refer to John 11:20-30 and explanin. _____

   _____

   _____

7. Explain the significance of Jesus' statements in John 11:25-26. What other statement of Jesus parallels this matter of death, the grave, and resurrection? _____

   _____

   _____

   _____

8. What faith do both Mary and Martha have about this situation? _____
_____

9. Even though Jesus knows the outcome of this trying situation, what is His reaction to the overwhelming grief? Make an application. _____
_____
_____

10. What are some of the thoughts of the bystanders before Lazarus appears?
_____
_____

11. Why would Jesus command the stone to be taken away and later command the grave clothes to be removed, and not do this Himself?_____
_____
_____

12. Jesus' prayer before this event is similar to another person's statement in this story. Whose?_____

13. What are the positive reactions to this miracle?_____
_____
_____

14. From John 11:47-54, the chief priests and the Pharisees have found themselves in a dilemma.

   A. What is it? _____
   _____

   B. What are some truths they've heard and remembered?_____
   _____

   C. What must Jesus do now? _____
   _____

Jesus starts the last journey to Jerusalem through Samaria and Galilee (Lk. 17:11-37)

1. Why does Jesus send the lepers to the priest? _____

2. What is unique about the thankful leper? _____

3. Explain Jesus' response to the Pharisees in Luke 17:20-21. _____

4. What do the disciples desire to see and why? _____

5. What does the reference to lightning represent? _____

6. Why do the examples of Noah and Lot illustrate Jesus' coming? _____

7. What might be the meaning of "one taken and one left?" _____

8. Explain Luke 17:37. _____

Parables on prayer (Lk. 18:1-14)

1. What lessons are learned from the parable in Luke 18:2-8? _____

2. What prompts the parable of Luke 18:10-14? _____
_____
_____

3. What is the purpose in using the terms "Pharisee" and "publican?" _____
_____
_____

4. What made the Pharisee's prayer unacceptable, or the publican's prayer acceptable? _____
_____

5. Make an application of both of these parables. _____
_____
_____

Jesus teaches on divorce (Matt. 19:1-12; Mk. 10:1-12)

1. Why would the Pharisees tempt Jesus with this question? _____
_____

2. What is the answer to the question? _____
_____

3. Where does Jesus point for the answer? _____
_____

4. Does the toleration mentioned of Moses have anything to do with the authority we are bound by today? Explain. _____
_____
_____

5. Who is exempt from God's law of marriage, divorce, and remarriage? Explain.
_____
_____
_____

6. Who is eligible to enter into a marriage relationship by Jesus' definition? _____

7. Who is ineligible to marry? _____

8. What does the disciples' statement, "If the case of man be so with his wife, it is not expedient to marry," indicate about their understanding of Jesus' teaching? _____

9. Does Jesus' statement in the last part of verse 11 and the last part of verse 12 mean that you do not have to receive this saying if you choose not to? Explain. _____

The spirit of children and the kingdom (Matt. 19:13-15; Mk. 10:13-16; Lk. 18:15-17)

1. What is the attitude of the disciples toward those who brought children to Jesus, and why? _____

2. How does Jesus identify the children with the kingdom? _____

3. Explain the way Jesus is saying a person should receive the kingdom? _____

The rich ruler, riches, and greatness (Matt. 19:16-20:16; Mk. 10:17-31; Lk. 18:18-30)

1. What are some positive things about this rich ruler's approach to Jesus? _____
   _____
   _____

2. What is said of Jesus' attitude about this man? What does this probably say about the motive of the rich ruler? _____
   _____

3. What does Matthew 19:20 reveal about this man's self-examination? _____
   _____

4. Why is it so hard for a rich man to enter the kingdom, and how does Jesus illustrate this? _____
   _____
   _____

5. What do the disciples recognize with the question "who then can be saved?"
   _____
   _____

6. In the context of the study, "who then can be saved," what does Jesus mean in Mark 10:27? _____
   _____

7. What does Jesus promise to those who forfeited all and followed Him? _____
   _____
   _____

8. Who are the characters of the parable in Matt. 20:1-16, and what essential point does it teach? _____
   _____
   _____

Jesus again foretells his death and resurrection and rebukes James and John (Matt. 20:17-28; Mk. 10:32-45; Lk. 18:31-34)

1. Why are the disciples afraid to go to Jerusalem, and do Jesus' words seem to comfort? _____
   _____
   _____

2. Who seems to be behind James and John, and what are they thinking about after Jesus departure? _____
   _____
   _____

3. About what does Jesus inform James and John? _____
   _____

4. What does the reaction of the ten reveal about the twelve as a whole? _____
   _____

5. How does Jesus define greatness? _____
   _____

Blind Bartimaeus (Matt. 20:29-34; Mk. 10:46-52; Lk. 18:35-43)

1. How many blind men are there? Harmonize all three accounts. _____
   _____
   _____

2. What things did Bartimaeus understand? _____
   _____
   _____

3. What produces the faith that makes the blind man whole? _____
   _____

Zacchaeus and the parable of the pounds (Lk. 19:1-28)

1. What are the good qualities of this man the others overlooked? _____
   _____
   _____

2. What might have been the motive for the murmuring of Luke 19:7? _____
   _____

3. What gives the impression that the kingdom was immediately present? _____
   _____

4. How does the parable of the pounds (Lk. 19:12-27) remedy the two issues stated in Luke 19:11? _____
   _____

Jesus arrives at Bethany—Friday, one week before crucifixion (Jn. 11:55-12:1, 9-11)

1. Aside from the impending death of the Lord in prophecy, why is Jesus going to Jerusalem? _____
   _____

2. What is the "talk of the town?" _____
   _____
   _____

The Last Public Ministry in Jerusalem

Jesus' triumphal entry into Jerusalem—Sunday before the crucifixion (Matt. 21:1-11, 14-17; Mk. 11:1-11; Lk. 19:29-44; Jn. 12:12-19)

1. What do you think is the point the Lord is making by choosing a young donkey to make His entrance into the city (besides fulfillment of prophecy)? _____
   _____
   _____

2. What do the multitudes do at the arrival of Jesus, and what does Hosanna mean?
   _____
   _____

3. What do the Pharisees say? Explain Luke 19:39-40. _____
   _____
   _____

4. What is Jesus referring to in Luke 19:42-44? _____
   _____
   _____

5. What event agitates the chief scribes and priests? _____
   _____
   _____

The barren fig tree cursed and the second cleansing of the temple—Monday before the crucifixion (Matt. 21:18, 19, 12, 13; Mk. 11:12-18; Lk. 19:45-48)

1. What might be a reason for Jesus cursing and withering the fig tree? _____
   _____
   _____

2. Cleaning the temple angers the chief priests and scribes. What statements express their feelings and others about Jesus, and why don't they lay hold on Him? _____

_____

_____

_____

Greeks are desiring to see Jesus—Monday before the crucifixion (Jn. 12:20-50)

1. What lesson is Jesus teaching in John 12:24-25? _____

_____

_____

2. What statement explains the mixed emotions Jesus is experiencing? _____

_____

_____

3. What is Jesus' primary concern, and how is verified? _____

_____

_____

4. What does Jesus mean in John 12:31? _____

_____

5. How does Jesus' words in John 12:35-36 answer the question asked of Him in John 12:34? _____

_____

6. What has Isaiah prophesied long before? _____

_____

_____

7. Briefly outline John 12:44-50. _____

_____

_____

LESSON 8 The Last Public Ministry in Jerusalem

Jesus speaks about the barren fig tree—Tuesday before the crucifixion (Matt. 21:19-22; Mk. 11:19-25)

1. What does Jesus use the fig tree to illustrate? _____

Jesus is challenged about His authority and teaches with more parables (Matt. 21:23-22:14; Mk. 11:27-12:12; Lk. 20:1-19)

1. How does Jesus answer their question about authority? _____

2. What problem ais Jesus' challengers faced with after His answer?_____

3. In Matthew 21:28-32, what is the conclusion of the chief priests and elders?_____

4. From Mark 12:1-11: who do the characters in this parable represent, and what lesson is Jesus teaching? _____

The Pharisees and Herodians try to ensnare Jesus about paying tribute to Caesar—Tuesday (Matt. 22:15-22; Mk. 12:13-17; Lk. 20:20-26)

1. What claims do these tempters make before Jesus? _____

2. What are these tempters really trying to do? _____

3. What lesson does this serve to teach today? _____

The Sadducees inquire of the resurrection—Tuesday (Matt. 22:23-33; Mk. 12:18-27; Lk. 20:27-40)

1. What do the Sadducees think they are doing with their mode of questioning, and of what does it remind you? _____
   _____
   _____

2. On what two counts does Jesus indict the Sadducees? Explain each one. _____
   _____
   _____
   _____

3. What/who does Jesus call to the record and how does He silence their ignorance?
   _____
   _____
   _____

The greatest commandment—Tuesday (Matt. 22:23-40; Mk. 12:28-34)

1. The two greatest commandments are summed up by what two relationships? _____
   _____
   _____

2. What does the statement, "on these two commandments hang the whole law and the prophets" mean? _____
   _____
   _____

3. What does Jesus recognize about the scribe who answered him? _____
   _____
   _____

The lineage/descent of Jesus and silencing of His enemies—Tuesday (Matt. 22:41-46; Mk. 12:35-37; Lk. 20:41-44)

1. Where does this teaching take place?_____

2. What questioning does Jesus use to confound these men, and what is their answer? Explain Jesus' reasoning. _____

Jesus denounces the Scribes and Pharisees in His last public discourse—Tuesday (Matt. 23:1-39; Mk. 12:38-40; Lk. 20:45-47)

1. In Matthew 23:1-5, what contrasts and observation about the Pharisees' works does Jesus make? Make a modern day application. _____

2. What problem does Matthew 23:6-12 address? Make a modern day application. _____

3. What social injustice does Jesus expose? _____

4. What is the "swearing" condemned by Jesus in Matthew 23:16-22? _____

5. Matthew 23:23-25 exposes another hypocrisy of these men, what is it?_____

6. What "real" problem does Jesus address with His remarks in Matthew 23:25-28?

86   A Harmony of the Gospels

7. What indictment of these men does Jesus make in Matthew 23:29-39, and what is the irony of this charge? _____

_____

_____

Jesus observes the contributions in the Temple—Tuesday (Mk. 12:41-44; Lk. 21:1-4)

1. What is the difference between the widow giving and the others? _____

_____

_____

The Lord's coming—Tuesday (Matt. 24 and 25; Mk. 13:1-37; Lk. 21:5-36)

1. There are typically three different schools of thought about these passages. What are they? _____

_____

_____

_____

2. What is the meaning of Jesus' response to the disciples' comments about the Temple's grandeur? _____

_____

_____

3. What questions do the disciples ask him? _____

_____

_____

4. What forms of speech in Matthew 24:4-29 demonstrate the time frame Jesus is referring? _____

_____

_____

LESSON 8 The Last Public Ministry in Jerusalem

5. What statements in Matthew 24:4-29 help determine the event Jesus is discussing? _____
_____
_____

6. What language of the Lord indicates he could be talking about a different subject in Matthew 24:29-35? Has changed themes? Explain your answer. _____
_____
_____
_____

7. How does the record of Noah tie into Jesus' teaching at this point? _____
_____
_____

8. What does the parable in Matthew 24:42-51 teach? To which viewpoint (question 1) do you think this parable is directed? _____
_____
_____

9. What does the parable of the virgins teach? To which viewpoint (question 1) do you think this parable is directed? _____
_____
_____

10. At this point Jesus introduces the parable of the talents. How can we connect the progression of these thoughts? _____
_____
_____

11. To what event do you ascribe Matthew 25:31-46? _____
_____

12. What lesson do we learn from Matthew 25:34-46? _____
_____

88 A Harmony of the Gospels

13. After studying these passages, what conclusions have you drawn and why? Explain your answer. _____

_____

_____

_____

Jesus predicts His crucifixion and is anointed with oil—Tuesday (Matt. 26:1-13; Mk. 14:1-9; Jn. 12:2-8)

1. Who are the "ringleaders" behind the plot to kill Jesus? _____

_____

2. Who anoints Jesus, and who is angry about her doing so? _____

_____

3. Why does she anoint Jesus, and what would be her legacy? _____

_____

_____

Judas was a part of the scheme—Tuesday (Matt. 26:14-16; Mk. 14:10-11; Lk. 22:3-6)

1. Who initiates the dialogue between Judas and the chief priests? What might have been the possible issue that triggered such a terrible deed by Judas? _____

_____

_____

_____

Lesson 9

The Last Few Days Before His Trial

The preparation and partaking of the Passover meal—Thursday evening, Jewish Friday (Matt. 26:17-25; Mk. 14:12-21; Lk. 22:7-23; Jn. 13:1-30)

1. How is the location to eat the Passover determined, and where is it? _____
   _____
   _____

2. Who is at the Passover meal with Jesus, and what statement reveals Jesus' anticipation about this? _____
   _____
   _____

3. What problem arises at the meal? _____
   _____

4. What does Jesus' statement in Luke 22:28-30 reveal? _____
   _____
   _____

5. How does "the devil put into the heart of Judas to betray Jesus?" (Jn. 13: 2-3) _____
   _____
   _____

6. What is the purpose of Jesus washing the disciples' feet? _____
   _____

7. What is Peter's attitude, and what is it that he does not know? (Jn. 13:7) _____
   _____
   _____

8. What is the example Jesus said He gave? _____
   _____
   _____

9. What does Jesus reveal while washing the disciples' feet? _____
   _____
   _____

10. Who do the disciples suspect is the betrayer? _____

11. What does Jesus tell Judas? _____
    _____

The departure of Judas and Jesus' warnings—Thursday evening, Jewish Friday (Matt. 26:31-35; Mk. 14:27-31; Lk. 22:31-38; Jn. 13:31-38)

1. In your own words, sum up what Jesus tells the 11 after the departure of Judas?
   _____
   _____

2. How are they "offended" as Jesus predicts? _____
   _____

3. What does Jesus say is the trademark of discipleship? _____
   _____

4. In what way will "all" the disciples be offended? Make a practical example. _____
   _____
   _____

5. Define Peter's problem. _____
   _____

6. In spite of Peter's tendencies, how does Jesus express optimism about him? _____
   _____
   _____

7. Explain Luke 22:35-38. _____

_____

_____

Jesus institues the memorial (Matt. 26:26-29; Mk. 14:22-25; Lk. 22:17-20)

1. Who is present with Jesus at this point? _____

_____

2. What is the significance of using unleavened bread and Jesus' statement, "Take, eat, this is my body?" _____

_____

_____

3. What are some parallels or thoughts you have about statements like "blood of the covenant," "drink ye all of it," and any other point regarding the fruit of the vine.

_____

_____

_____

4. From 1 Corinthians 11:23-26, list points of interest that Paul reveals which are not mentioned in the Gospel accounts (Note that Paul was not present at Jesus' institution of this). _____

_____

_____

The farewell discourse in the upper room—Thursday (Jn. 14, 15, and 16)

Let's remember as we study these chapters that this is the last discourse to His disciples (would-be Apostles), other than some prayer time together. Given this, let's try to consider this setting in the context of our study of these statements.

1. Why are the hearts of the disciples troubled, and how does Jesus offer comfort?

_____

_____

92   A Harmony of the Gospels

2. What is Thomas' problem and what is Jesus' answer? Make an application. _____
   _____
   _____
   _____

3. Explain Jesus' statement in John 14:6. _____
   _____
   _____

4. Jesus' answer to Philip's question reveals his problem. What is it? _____
   _____
   _____

5. Explain Jesus' statement in John 14:11. _____
   _____
   _____

6. Given the context of these statements, what is the significance of John 14:15? Also, from these three chapters, list the other occasions where the Lord emphasizes this same point. _____
   _____
   _____
   _____

7. From various statements in these three chapters, what is the Comforter, what is He to do, and what will He prove? _____
   _____
   _____

8. How does Jesus answer Judas' question? _____
   _____

9. In your own words, explain John 14:27 in light of life's ever-present conflicts. _____
   _____
   _____

LESSON 9 The Last Few Days Before His Trial

10. Why is Jesus declaring these things to the disciples? _____
_____

11. List as many points from John 15:1-10 regarding the "vine and the branches," and define the different metaphors in the illustration (i.e. Jesus is the vine). _____
_____
_____

12. In John 15:11, Jesus reveals the things just stated are "that my joy might remain in you." Explain. _____
_____
_____

13. How does Jesus describe great love and what is the contingency for being His friend? _____
_____
_____

14. From these three chapters, list the verses where Jesus discusses love. What's the point? _____
_____
_____

15. What distinction is Jesus making in John 15:15? _____
_____
_____

16. What is Jesus' purpose from His statements in John 15:18-25? _____
_____

17. From John 16:1-6, what must the disciples conclude, and what statement of Jesus reveals this? _____
_____
_____

18. How are the disciples confused by Jesus in John 15:16, and what is Jesus' answer?
___
___
___

19. Go back through these three chapters and list the verses that compare with John 16:23-24. ___
___

20. When would the fulfillment of John 16:25 be realized? ___
___

21. What confidence does Jesus have in the disciple's understanding? ___
___

22. Explain John 16:32. ___
___
___

The Lord's prayer (Jn. 17:1-26)

1. Outline the prayer. ___
___
___
___

2. List the things that Jesus states in this prayer that He has done. ___
___
___

3. Who does Jesus pray for in this prayer (specifically)? ___
___

4. Who is the "son of perdition?" ___

5. How are the disciples to be "set apart?" _____
   _____
   _____

6. How is perfection (completeness) achieved? _____
   _____
   _____

Lesson 10

The Arrest, Trial, Crucifixion and Burial of Jesus

Going to Gethsemane—Late Thursday night, Jewish Friday (Matt. 26:30, 36-46; Mk. 14:26, 32-32-42; Lk. 22:39-46; Jn. 18:1)

1. What habit of Jesus is mentioned in these texts? _____

2. Who (how many) go with Jesus to the Garden? (You must read ahead of the above texts to answer this.) _____

3. What is Jesus' disposition at this time? Explain. _____

4. What is the substance of Jesus' prayers, and how many times does He return to the disciples? Explain. _____

5. What does the statement, "the spirit indeed is willing, but the flesh is weak" mean? _____

6. What does the Lord finally tell them to do? _____

Jesus is betrayed, arrested, and forsaken—Friday before dawn (Matt. 26:47-56; Mk. 14:43-52; Lk. 22:47-53; Jn. 18:2-12)

1. Who is leading the vigilante arrest squad, where does he get his "marching orders," and how does he know where to bring them? _____
   _____
   _____

2. What is the irony of the fact that they brought weapons to apprehend Jesus? _____
   _____
   _____

3. What happens upon the arrival of the vigilante arrest squad? _____
   _____

4. What is the trick Judas uses and why? _____
   _____

5. Jesus exerts His divine power one last time prior to His resurrection. How? _____
   _____
   _____

6. What prophesies are fulfilled in these texts? _____
   _____
   _____

7. How do the disciples react? _____
   _____

The first examination—Friday before dawn (Jn. 18:12-14, 19-23)

1. What is Caiaphas' judgment, and what does he ask Jesus? _____
   _____
   _____

2. What is Jesus accused of? _____
   _____

LESSON 10 The Arrest, Trial, Crucifixion and Burial of Jesus   99

The second examination—Early Friday morning
(Matt. 26:57, 59-68; Mk. 14:53, 55-65; Lk. 22:54, 63-65; Jn. 18:24)

1. Where is Jesus led, who is present, and for what do they contend? _____
   _____
   _____

2. What are the charges brought against Jesus, and what is the problem with the witnesses? _____
   _____
   _____

3. How does Jesus respond? _____
   _____

4. What is the reaction to Jesus' response? _____
   _____

Peter's denial—Early Friday morning (Matt. 26:58, 69-75; Mk. 14:54, 66-72; Lk. 22:54-62; Jn. 18:15-18, 25-27)

1. Where has Peter been up to this point, what has he been doing, and what is he asked? _____
   _____
   _____

2. What statement shows the tenacity of Peter's denial? _____
   _____

3. What statement shows the proximity of Peter to Jesus in this setting? _____
   _____

Jesus is formally condemned by the Sanhedrin—Daylight Friday
(Matt. 27:1; Mk. 15:1; Lk. 22:66-71)

1. On what point do they finally agree to condemn Jesus? _____
   _____

Judas commits suicide—Friday morning (Matt. 27:3-10)

1. What triggers Judas' remorse? _____
   _____

2. What is the attitude of those whom he aided? _____
   _____

3. What becomes of the money that Judas received for the betrayal? _____
   _____

Jesus before Pilate the first time—Friday morning (Matt. 27:2, 11-14; Mk. 15:1-5; Lk. 23:1-5; Jn. 18:28-38)

1. What strategy do they use to accuse Jesus before Pilate, and what is Pilate's first statement? _____
   _____
   _____

2. Explain the significance of John 18:31b-32. _____
   _____
   _____

3. What does Pilate ask Jesus, why might he be asking, and how does Jesus respond?
   _____
   _____
   _____

4. What point(s) can learned from John 18:36? _____
   _____
   _____

5. What accusations do the enemies of Jesus persist with? _____
   _____

6. In what spirit or attitude do you think Pilate asks the question in John. 18:38?
   _____

LESSON 10 The Arrest, Trial, Crucifixion and Burial of Jesus

Jesus before Herod the Tetrarch—Friday morning (Lk. 23:6-12)

1. How would you describe Herod's thoughts about Jesus before meeting him? After?
   _____
   _____
   _____

Jesus before Pilate the second time—Friday morning (Matt. 27:15-26; Mk. 15:6-16; Lk. 23:13-25; Jn. 18:39-19:16)

1. There is one opportunity that Jesus could have had to be released. What was it, and what happened? _____
   _____

2. What is Pilate's judgment about Jesus this time, and what does he suggest? _____
   _____
   _____

3. What does Pilate's wife think? _____
   _____

4. Who do they want released? _____

5. What do the soldiers do with Jesus and how does Pilate's express his attitude?____
   _____
   _____

6. To what penal code do the Jews say they live by, and what accusation against Jesus is their basis for crucifying Jesus? _____
   _____

7. What passages show Pilate's fear and frustrations, how does Jesus respond, and what political pressure do the Jews apply to Pilate? _____
   _____
   _____
   _____

8. After Pilate consents to releasing Jesus to be killed, what does Pilate do before the multitude? _____

The Roman soldiers mock Jesus—Friday morning (Matt. 27:27:30; Mk. 15:16-19)

1. Take these two accounts and list all the events as they occurred. _____
   _____
   _____
   _____

Jesus on the way to the cross—9 a.m. Friday morning (Matt. 27:31-34; Mk. 15:20-23; Lk. 23:26-33; Jn. 19:16-17)

1. Why might it have been necessary for Simon of Cyrene to bear Jesus' cross? _____
   _____

2. What does Jesus mean by His statements to the women in John 23:28-31? _____
   _____
   _____

3. Who else is in the procession with Jesus? _____
   _____

4. What is the significance of the wine mixed with gall? _____
   _____
   _____

The first three hours on the cross—9 a.m. to 12 p.m. Friday (Matt. 27:35-44; Mk. 15:24-32; Lk. 23:33-43; Jn. 19:18-27)

1. Who wrote the inscription "King of the Jews?" _____

2. What do the soldiers do at this point? _____
   _____

LESSON 10 The Arrest, Trial, Crucifixion and Burial of Jesus 103

3. What three statements does Jesus make in the above texts, and what is the nature of these statements? _____

_____

_____

4. What statements are made to Jesus? _____

_____

_____

5. Explain the discourse between Jesus and the thieves. List any significant points to be learned. _____

_____

_____

_____

6. Discuss John 19:25-27. _____

_____

_____

The next three hours on the cross (Matt. 27:45-50; Mk. 15:33-37; Lk. 23:44-46)

1. What supernatural event happens in this time period? Do you have an explanation?

_____

_____

2. List four sayings of Jesus found in these texts, and give a phrase that describes each one. _____

_____

_____

The phenomena at the death of Jesus (Matt. 27:51-56; Mk. 15:38-41; Lk. 23: 45, 47-49)

1. What are the phenomena? _____

_____

2. What is the reaction to these miracles? _____
   _____

The burial of Jesus (Matt. 27:57-60; Mk. 15:42-46; Lk. 23:50-54; Jn. 19:31-42)

1. Why is the request made to break the legs of the crucified, and why are Jesus' legs not broken? _____
   _____

2. Who asks for the body of Jesus, and what is said of him? _____
   _____

3. Who helps with the preparation of the body for burial? _____
   _____

4. Where do they bury Jesus, and what is the significance? _____
   _____
   _____

The watch of the tomb (Matt. 27:61-28:1; Lk. 23:55-56; Mk. 15:47-16:1)

1. Who watches the tomb and for how long? _____
   _____

2. What do the Pharisees request, and what is done? _____
   _____

3. Harmonize the alleged contradiction between Matthew 28:1 and Mark 16:1. ____
   _____
   _____

Lesson 11

The Resurrection, Appearances and Ascension of Christ

Early Sunday morning (Matt. 28:2-4; Mk. 16:2-8; Lk. 24:1-8; Jn. 20:1)

1. Who arrives at the tomb, and what do they find? _____
_____
_____

2. List the things these first visitors are informed of, and list the ways these messengers are described. _____
_____
_____

3. What comes to the minds of these visitors? _____
_____

The report of the resurrection (Lk. 24:9-12; Jn. 20:2-10)

1. Compare the accounts. Who is given the report of Jesus' resurrection, and what is the reaction? _____
_____
_____

2. Who goes to the tomb at this point, and what is found? _____
_____
_____

Jesus appears to Mary Magdalene (Mk. 16:9-11; Jn. 20:11-18)

1. What are Mary's initial thoughts? _____
_____
_____

2. Explain Jesus' statements in John 20:17-18. _____
   _____
   _____

3. What does the Lord commission her to do? _____
   _____

The appearance of Jesus to the other women, and the report of the guards (Matt. 28:9-15)

1. What are the disciples instructed to do and what might be a possible explanation?
   _____
   _____
   _____

2. What do the guards initially report and to whom? _____
   _____
   _____

3. What is the plan, and why do some think it is needed? _____
   _____
   _____

Jesus appears to two more disciples, and their report (Mk. 16:12-13; Lk. 24:13-35)

1. What miracle does Jesus perform in this encounter? _____
   _____

2. What problem does Jesus recognize in these men? _____
   _____
   _____

3. What is the reaction of these men after the encounter? _____
   _____

4. Who were the two disciples? _____

LESSON 11 The Resurrection, Appearances and Ascension of Christ

The appearance to the disciples (Lk. 24:36-43; Jn. 20:19-25)

1. What is the disciple's reaction, and with what are they having a difficult time? _____

2. What is the first thing Jesus attempts to establish, how does He do it, and what is its significance? _____

3. What further evidence does Jesus set forth? _____

4. How would the disciples forgive sins? _____

5. How is Thomas different than the other disciples? _____

The appearance with Thomas (Jn. 20:26-31)

1. What are the disciples found doing at this time? _____

2. What event signals to a disciple that it is Jesus on the shore? What does this infer? _____

3. What does the Lord press Peter for? _____

4. What does Jesus reveal to Peter? _____

5. What is Peter concerned with? _____

_____

The great commission (Matt. 28:16-20; Mk. 16:15-18; Lk. 24:44-49)

1. Where does this setting take place, and what is the disposition of some? _____

_____

_____

2. What is the first premise Jesus establishes before commissioning them? _____

_____

_____

3. What is the significance of "go ye?" _____

_____

4. Explain who the believers are in Mark 16:17-18? _____

_____

5. What does Jesus open their mind to understand? _____

_____

6. What are significant points to be learned from Luke 24:46-49? _____

_____

_____

The last appearance and ascension of our Lord (Mk. 16:19-20; Lk. 24:50-53; Acts 1:4-11)

1. What is the nature of the disciples after witnessing this event? _____

_____

2. What is the difference between the so-called miracle workers of today and that of Mark 16:20? _____

_____

www.ingramcontent.com/pod-product-compliance
Lightning Source LLC
Chambersburg PA
CBHW081357040426
42451CB00018B/3489